SPIRITUAL WISDOM
For
ENTREPRENEURS

SPIRITUAL WISDOM
For
ENTREPRENEURS

Reaching Your Full Potential in Entrepreneurship

Dr. Patrick W. Sanders Sr.

Elevate Publishing
billing@elevatemastercoaching.com

Ordering Information:
Quantity sales. Special discounts are available on quantity purchases by corporations, associations, and others. For details, contact eldersanders@att.net.

Printed in the United States of America

Publisher's Cataloging-in-Publication data
Sanders Sr., Dr. Patrick W.

A title of a book: Spiritual Wisdom for Entrepreneurs / Dr. Patrick W. Sanders Sr.
p. cm.

ISBN 978-0-9978898-7-1

1. The main category of the book —Business —Self Help.
2. Spirituality

First Edition

14 13 12 11 10 / 10 9 8 7 6 5 4 3 2 1

Dedication

This book is dedicated to my 2 fathers Leon Sanders and Johnny Davenport. I have been incredibly blessed to have 2 fathers who nurtured me throughout the years and helped me to be the man and entrepreneur I am today. Both of my father's were great men who taught me a lot about work ethic and smart hustle. I pray this book and my life is a testament to their love. Rest in Peace, your son Patrick.

CONTENTS

Introduction

Why did I decide to write this book? Why would I even embark on such a journey? Well, the truth is that I love the spirit of entrepreneurship with a passion. Something about it wakes me up every day, and something about it drives my innermost person to want to be the master of my own world. When I say that, I mean no disrespect to God, of course, but I did not want my future to be in someone else's hands. So, for years I have always wanted to be my own boss, so to speak… do my own thing, and help empower others. I discovered that the best way to do that, or the quickest and most impactful way to do that is to be an entrepreneur. I watched my dad for years, and like most young men from my era, I wanted to be like him. He was a passionate and dedicated produce delivery guy, who was able to make money by working deals for other. He hustled to make sure that our family had what we needed. His way of conducting business struck a chord with me, leaving a big impression on my life. Although, I did not particularly embrace all his principles, I got the entrepreneurial bug. Within the past 50 years, I have started many businesses, most of which were not successful. However, the businesses that were successful was due to spiritual wisdom I learned, and all entrepreneurs can follow. I am writing this book in hopes that it will inspire and encourage all of you to be great.

The Wisdom of Vision

"Good business leaders create a vision, articulate the vision, passionately own the vision, and relentlessly drive it to completion."

— Jack Welch

Parable of Three Fish- Unknown

Once up on a time, there lived three fish in a pond: Plan Ahead, Think Fast, and Wait and See. One day, they heard a fisherman say that he was going to cast his net in their pond the next day.

Plan Ahead said, "I am swimming down the river tonight!" Then, he did so.

Think Fast said, "I am sure I will come up with a plan."

Wait and See lazily said, "I just can't think about it now!"

When the fisherman cast his nets, Plan Ahead was long gone, but Think Fast and Wait and See were both caught!

Think Fast quickly rolled up his belly and pretended to be dead. The fisherman declared, "Oh, this fish is no good!" and threw him safely back into the water. However, Wait and See ended up in the fish market.

The old saying goes, "In times of danger, when the net is cast, plan ahead or plan to think fast!"

Moral: One should have vision, which helps with planning ahead and avoiding dangerous circumstances.

A vision is a picture, idea, or wish that you have in your mind about yourself, business, family or anything that could happen in the future. A sharp vision helps you pursue dreams and achieve goals, and it will open your mind to endless possibilities.

A vision will help you overcome roadblocks and hold on when times are tough. If well-defined, it can help you focus and create purpose that will become your measurement for success. If you do not have vision of who you want to be, how you want to succeed, or what you want out of life, you will lack drive, and your life will only be an order of events.

A strong vision connects with your passions and greatest potentials. Regardless of world events or challenges, vision will set you on the path of success. You will feel much more valuable as a person when you set and achieve visions and goals.

The Importance of a Vision

A vision can be viewed in two ways: inspiration and prediction. It inspires you to reach certain goals. Also, it is used to predict changes in the future. A vision might be the most powerful way to stay focused on goals while remaining motivated to achieve them. It will open your mind to many possibilities and a brighter and bigger future. When you can envision a future that is better, happier, and more productive, you are more likely to make necessary changes.

Vision and Entrepreneurship

When an entrepreneur has vision, they can see today as it is and calculate a future business that will grow and continuously improve. A successful entrepreneur can see the future while remaining focused on present business matters. For this individual, vision is not a dream, but rather reality that has not come into existence. Vision is easily perceived for entrepreneurs because their dedication and confidence are extremely strong. Determined entrepreneurs spend hours upon hours bringing their visions to reality. Their vision acts as a driving force within them to create a sustainable business.

However dear friends, vision is not without issues for entrepreneurs. The main issue is communicating the vision for their business to people who will help move it forward successfully. This is difficult because vision is clear for the person who receives it but not necessarily for others around them. However, a successful entrepreneur can relay the vision to their team in such a way that it comes to life. This is a must for successful entrepreneurship.

Another issue is the discouragement that comes from those who do not understand your vision. My question to you though is, "Who told you?"

Who told you that you could not start that business or that idea won't work? Who told you that you cannot receive that loan, or no one will buy your product or service? Who told you these things? More importantly, why are you listening?

Successful entrepreneurs understand that they must shut out all the white noise and follow their vision. Naysayers are people who have placed you in a very small box and try to contain you, mainly because it is comfortable for them. However, today, as you are look forward and read this book, it is my prayer that you break out of the box they tried to put you in and begin entertaining a world of possibilities.

People question your vision because they think small and do not understand it. They may say things like, "You are not smart enough." "You are not good enough." "You do not have what it takes to start and own a business." "You do not have what it takes to be your own boss." "You do not have what it takes to make a difference in your community or in the life of a young person."

Who told you? It is this question that is important.

God himself, the God of the universe --- and if I come off preachy, perhaps it is because that is what I do for a living --- that's who told you. That is from whom the vision ultimately comes. So, the question is this, if God gave you the vision, and God is the one who told you, then why do you listen and react to the naysayers?

"What, then, shall we say in response to these things? If God is for us, who can be against us?" Romans 8:31

Let us look at a well-known story in the Bible. In Genesis, the Bible tells us that God would meet with and talk to Adam every day in the garden at the cool of the evening. One day, God came down at the same time as usual, but Adam is nowhere to be found. So, God began to call out to Adam. God said, "Adam, where art thou?", to which Adam does not respond. Bishop T. D. Jakes says, "Anytime that God asks a question, he is not asking for his own knowledge. He is asking so that you will know that He knows the answer already." After a while, Adam finally replied, saying, "I heard you coming, and I was naked." Then, God asked an amazing question to His creation, "Who told you were naked?"

This question has resonated in my spirit and my heart for the entrepreneur. Who told you? Who told you that you could not get this done, and why did you believe them? Adam suffered from something that, unfortunately, we all do. Once we have been told that we have limitations, we then become paralyzed by what we have heard the opposition say. When negative things are heard, the human spirit immediately goes into belief mode. Then, it sets up a mental block, which says, "This is far as I can go." It is an old adage. It is the old syndrome that I have heard throughout American culture where we use negative and derogatory words that say, "You are just like your father." However, these words are not uplifting. They tear down rather than build up.

When you allow people to speak to you about your vision, you are putting them in a position of authority. This could grant them authority over your life, and you must be able to determine whether you are going to give them this space to operate in.

Who told you? Who said it about you? When you determine the authoritative figure in your life that is not God, then you can break the chain in your life and begin again. When will you begin to push forward with the vision that God gave you? That's all God was asking Adam, "Who told you were naked?" And when you believe them, you empower them in your life.

If this describes your experience, it should be your goal to unplug from these people and redirect your energy into positive, affirming people. You will then be able to become the great entrepreneur that the God of the universe has designed you to be.

Successful entrepreneurs, like Steve Jobs, dealt with many naysayers. He had people close to him who could not see his vision. They thought he did not have what it took; they even thought he was crazy at times. These naysayers had no problem telling this visionary that he could not cut it. They even kicked him out of the very company that he had built from the ground up. Imagine that! Yet, Steve, at some point in his journey, decided that he would no longer buy into what others said success should look like. He was right, because they eventually called him back run his company. Steve Jobs left a legacy for all entrepreneurs to follow. He followed his vision, and we must do the same. We must work our vision exactly as God has given it to us. We must do so with wild abandon like Steve Jobs, leaving our naysayers in the distance. So, whether you have five employees, just one, or 5,000, be good to yourself and strive to be the best. Just do not do it based on the standards of others.

This requires time with your Creator and pen and paper to write the vision. Make it plain. Learn your vision, who you are, what makes you happy, and what you have to offer. Steve Jobs is quoted as saying, "I want to leave a dent in the universe." What? A dent in the universe? I can imagine that on many occasions he was asked, "Who told you?" He did, in fact, put a dent in the universe. So, the final question then is not who told you, but instead, will you?

Reflection Time

1. How do you define vision in your own life?

2. How can vision help you build your business and

make you a successful entrepreneur?

Reflect on the times someone questioned your vision. How did you handle it? How would you handle it today?

What is your plan to eliminate the white noise and naysayers in your life?

The Wisdom of
Answering of the Call

*"God did not direct His call to Isaiah—
Isaiah overheard God saying, '. . . who
will go for Us?' The call of God is not just
for a select few, but for everyone. Whether
I hear God's call or not depends on the
condition of my ears, and exactly what I
hear depends upon my spiritual attitude."*

— Oswald Chambers

After preaching for 30 years, I must admit that I have experienced answering the call many times. What I have discovered is that the ultimate call is from God himself, given to each of us before we were even created. It is an assignment…a special assignment for each person to fulfill in their lives. When I first heard God call me, I did not answer. I did not want to do whatever it was that God was calling me to do. I thought that God himself had made a mistake. In fact, I ran for several years before I really accepted my call to preaching. Again, I did not want to do it. Like most of us, I had other plans in place.

My plans were centered around having a career in travel and tourism. I was in Texas seeking a degree, but God himself had another plan. How true is Proverbs 16:9

that says, "We can make our plans, but the LORD determines our steps."

Yet, I ran. Then, I ran some more. I made a mess by not immediately answering the call and ruined some things in my life. Some things did not work out the way that I had planned. During this period, I learned if you do not answer God's call, He has a tendency of making you pay in your current state. What do I mean by that? Well, I have travelled to many places, but none of that would fulfil me. I eventually realized that my completion and fulfillment were attached to my calling.

Whether you are called to make pastries, become a barber, or run your own restaurant; at some point you must answer the call. To answer that call, you must be willing to take on all the responsibilities that come with it. The ridicule, the praise, the ups and the downs. That is where I found myself.

Truthfully, I ended up answering the call one night at a major party I was hosting in my three-story townhouse. The party had been going on for several days. People were everywhere, and it was a mess. For three days, I had found myself totally inebriated. Amid all the people and partying, God stepped in my bedroom, and I was instantaneously sober. I heard the voice like I had never heard anything else, simply saying, "I have had enough, and I want you to do what I have called you to do. I have had enough." Then silence. Like a light coming on in a dark alley, I found myself on the side of the dresser, kneeling and crying my eyes out because I had heard the voice of God speak to me. I came to myself and things would never be the same again. It was unbelievable.

Thus, I began my journey of answering the call and experiencing the troubles that would come with my calling. Do not let anyone convince you that by simply answering your calling that everything will be rosy. That is not the case here. Some days will be filled with hell, heartache, and hurt. You are going to experience disappointment, letdowns, will be hurt by some of the very people that you call your friends. That is a part of the call.

If you're going to be an entrepreneur, you must get used to walking the floor. You must get used to planning and strategizing, understanding people and how the process is going to work. You must be able to listen to the voice of God and hear him succinctly and clearly. Then, you must be able to hear him without interruption. As an entrepreneur, you will also have to learn how to listen to your inner voice. You will have to learn how to trust this voice and understand what is going on in the season. It is a call that has allowed you to be who you are. The more you embrace the call, the better off you will be. God controls something that you and I don't, and that is time. God has all the time in the world, and you and I are not that privileged. We have a limited space in time that He has permitted to us. By not accepting the call, you waste precious time, chasing after things that will never be yours because you're not listening to what His voice is saying. And so, most of us spend years trying to be something that we were never called to, and we were assuming positions that were never ours in the first place.

Let me be very clear that being called simply means that God has set you aside for His use. For His use.

Os Guinness states:

"Do we enjoy our work, love our work, virtually worship our work so that our devotion to Jesus is off-center? Do we put our emphasis on service, usefulness, or being productive in working for God—at his expense? Do we strive to prove our own significance? To make a difference in the world? To carve our names in marble on the monuments of time? The call of God blocks the path of all such deeply human tendencies. We are not primarily called to do something or go somewhere; we are called to Someone. We are not called to special work but to God. The key to answering the call is to be devoted to no one and to nothing above God himself. "

You want to be where God can use you. For those that do not want to be used, you are wasting your time. You are wasting your time telling God no because at the end of the day, He is going to get a yes. You can waste your time telling Him, "That's not what I want to do," but at the end of the day, we are all going to have to surrender to the will of God. You may say, "Pastor, you do not understand. I do not want to do it. I do not feel that is what I am called for."

Well, God is not asking you to feel. He is asking you to walk by faith. Hear His voice and strike out on the journey.

Once you accept where God has called you to serve, your life becomes a much clearer. Once you accept it for what it is, He makes easy the path that you should take. Easier, not trouble free.

Ring, Ring! Answer the call. Your phone is ringing. Will somebody please answer the phone? I would like to tell you that it is destiny on the other end of the call. Your purpose has dialed your phone number. Finally, your breakthrough is looking for you, and the only way you are going to get it is by answering the call. Life is calling. God is speaking and wanting to talk to you about your purpose and destiny. Your time is at hand.

I was looking for purpose. One day while traveling and trying to figure out who I was, the phone in my heart rang out. I picked it up, and lo and behold, what was on the other end of the phone when I said hello? It said my name, and I said, "Excuse me? Who are you looking for?" They repeated my name again. I asked, "Who's calling?", and they said, "It is destiny. It is purpose. It is chance and opportunity. It is what you have been looking for. I have finally called you to say to you that your destiny is at hand. Your purpose is at hand. Your future is now at hand. You have paid the price. Now receive the reward that you been looking for. Greater is what you are going to get. All because you finally took the initiative to answer the call that was on your life.

Reflection Time

1. When did God call you? What are you called to do?

2. What is your plan to execute the calling on your life?

The Wisdom of Identity

"When I discover who I am, I'll be free."

— Ralph Ellison, Invisible Man

"To know thyself is the beginning of wisdom." This famous quote is often attributed to Socrates. However, what exactly do you know when you "know yourself?" As you live your daily life, you can look for clues to these important building blocks of the self.

First, why is it important to know yourself?

Identity is not only knowing the name and details. It is about knowing who you really are, at the core, once all the masks that were placed to accommodate society fall off.

Funny enough, this is played out and forgotten so often in our daily lives that we have forgotten the significance of self-discovery. Life suddenly seems boring, empty and meaningless. And whatever role we have convinced ourselves to play, that of a husband/wife/boss/employee, etc., seems unfulfilling.

We have been sleepwalking all our lives, and, suddenly, we have been jolted awake into asking, "Who am I? What is my identity?" Then, the search begins for a deeper, more meaningful role to play in life. Once this question starts nagging us, nothing but authenticity will suffice.

Importance of Self-Identity for Happiness

Some, I am sure, will wonder why knowing ourselves is so important. Many find it irrelevant and put answering this question off. However, ask anyone who has been successful and happy about the degree of importance that self-knowledge has played in their lives.

Self-knowledge leads to self-mastery. Self-mastery empowers you to self-govern. Self-governance means that you are in total control of your mind and your emotional center, which ensures that you respond to situations and deal with them constructively to:

1) Get rid of negativity and stress in your life.

2) Become a better problem solver.

3) Have a positive work-life balance.

Importance of Self Identity for Success

Also, once we know our authentic selves, it is easier for us to find our purpose. Having a well-defined purpose gives us direction for success.

Those who have not been very successful in their lives are, often, unaware of their strengths are applying them elsewhere.

"Your work is to discover your world and then with all your heart give yourself to it" – Gautam Buddha

Why is it that we wait for an accident or a mishap to occur in our lives to jolt us into asking this most fundamental question? God, in His wisdom, ensures that a child develops a sense of self as early as the age of two. This process of developing self-identity lasts until a child is seven. Piaget calls this the pre-operational stage. The term pre-operational itself is suggestive of a stage that must be experienced before a person gets operational. What happens in this stage can either make or break the process.

The importance of this question is realized in our lives when we embark on new ventures. When you are starting a new business, you must know who you are as well as the identity of your business. Your identity as a person will be the foundation of your business and the substance of your brand. What is a brand, you may ask? Branding is simply the promise of an experience. Most people talk about branding as if it's only about the logo, the colors on your business sign or the look of your business overall. However, a legit brand promises customers' an experience. Where does that experience come from? Well it comes from you. As an entrepreneur, you are your brand and if you don't know who you are then your customers won't know who you are either. I have known many people who failed in their business endeavors because they were not rooted in their identity. As a result, they presented themselves and their business in a chaotic fashion. They changed their mission, services and products constantly and no knew what they were truly selling. Don't let this be you.

I implore you, future entrepreneur to spend time understanding who you are. Spend time understanding your values and your purpose. When you know your identity, branding will be easy. Presenting your product and services will be easy. Success won't be that far behind.

So, WHO ARE YOU?

Reflection Time

1. What is your identity? Who are you?

2. Ask 5 people close to you what your personal brand is. Compare their feedback to what you believe your own brand to be.

The Wisdom of Giving

"I believe that we all have a responsibility to give back. No one becomes successful without lots of demanding work, support from others, and a little luck. "Giving back creates a virtuous cycle that makes everyone more successful."

— Ron Conway

One day traveler was traveling through a distant village. On his way through the village he encountered a very poor old woman drawing water from a well. He stopped to talk to the woman because he noticed she wore a beautiful jeweled necklace. He thought how out of place this seemed since she was clearly very poor. The traveler began to talk to the old woman, and he asked her about her beautiful necklace. The old woman told the traveler the necklace was her grandmother's necklace and how its beauty brought her such joy.

The two sat and talked several hours, the old woman about life, family and more prosperous times, while the traveler spoke of his desire to become a Master with many students. During the entire conversation, the traveler couldn't keep his mind off the old woman's necklace. He thought to himself about how much money he could sell the necklace for. He thought about how he could easily purchase a school and live comfortably for many years. He thought, this old woman is nice enough, but why does she need such a precious possession. Afterall, she had not used it to make her life better. She had a beautiful necklace, but she was still poor. So as the traveler bid the old woman goodbye, he couldn't resist asking the old woman if he could have her necklace. Without a second thought, the old woman took off her necklace and handed it to the traveler. She asked him to accept it as a gift. The traveler was absolutely in disbelief, so he quickly bid the old woman goodbye and began on his way.

When the traveler reached his destination, a city of vast riches and prosperity. The traveler should have been happy to have reached such a beautiful place and to start his new life, but he couldn't help but think about the old woman. So, after being in the new city for 2 weeks with no motivation to start his school or sell the necklace, he decided to return to the old woman's village. When he got to the village, he found the old woman at the same well, drawing water the same as when they first met. The old woman was so surprised to see the traveler had returned. She greeted him warmly, but noticed he seemed different. The traveler then handed the old woman the necklace, the gift she gave him. The old woman asked the traveler about why he was returning the necklace. The traveler responded by saying, "I want to give you this necklace as payment." "As payment for what?" the old woman asked. Traveler responded by saying, "Master, please teach me what is inside of you that allowed you to give your most precious gift, the necklace away to me". - Unknown

A gift opens the way and ushers the giver into the presence of the great. And in business it does even more. For example, as an entrepreneur, giving connects you with the community and can also provide a much-needed tax break.

Look, I believe in charity. I have personally seen what happens when those who are able to give back do so. Communities are changed and lives are made better. What better way to show thanks to your patrons than to give back to those who invest in you and your business day in and day out.

Many great entrepreneurs understand the concept of giving back. According to a survey backed by Ernst & Young and conducted by Australia's Fidelity Charitable Gift Trust, 89 percent of entrepreneurs donate to charity. An additional 70 percent donate their time as well. If a company is led by an entrepreneur, their charitable giving is on average more than double of their peers who are not. Let us look at some who are extremely successful and make it a point to graciously give back.

Mark Zuckerberg- The Zuckerbergs regularly top the charts of the most giving entrepreneurs. In 2013, they donated $1 billion (yes, with a "B") to the Silicon Valley Community Foundation via company stock. Known for setting a fitting example as an entrepreneur and a philanthropist at a young age, the 29-year-olds have been moving Facebook shares over to non-profits for the past several years.

Phil and Penelope Knight- As co-founder of Nike, Mr. Knight targets Oregon-based organizations. He donated $500 million to Oregon Health & Science University (OHSU) in 2013, after OHSU asked "boldly" for $100 million. After seeing the incredible work being done, Knight shocked the non-profit teaching hospital by drastically upping the gift.

Mark Cuban- You might know Mark Cuban, the American businessman and owner of the Dallas Mavericks, from his appearances on the television show "Shark Tank," but you might not be familiar with his philanthropic work. In 2003, Cuban started the Fallen Patriot Fund to help families of United States military personnel killed or injured during Operation Iraqi Freedom. Cuban matched the first one million dollars in contributions with funds from the Mark Cuban Foundation, which is run by Mark's brother Brian Cuban, but does not directly operate any charitable activities. Rather, the Mark Cuban foundation supports charitable activities in the Dallas area and throughout the United States. Cuban is also reported to give freely to other charitable organizations.

These successful entrepreneurs understand that giving back is more than PR or just a tax write-off. They understand their responsibility to the greater good. Now, these are high profile people, so think about your regular everyday entrepreneurs who give back. They are in your neighborhood, your churches, and at local schools. Take the examples of the high profile and local entrepreneurs and create your own giving model. The wisdom in giving is that you get so much out of it. There is pure joy in giving….an investment that keeps on giving.

Personally, I believe I have a civic duty. I believe that it is my duty to pay it forward and help those who are less fortunate. It motivates me in both my personal and business lives. Yes, there are tax benefits to giving back, but I believe there are far greater business reasons. Even if this were not so, I would still give back because I believe it is the right thing to do. It is good for my soul, and it can be good for yours too. I give back so that I can go forward successfully.

Reflection Time

1. What do you feel your responsibility is as it relates to giving?

2. Think of some charitable organizations that align with your personal and business goals. What can you do to get involved?

The Wisdom of Collaboration/Community

"And let us consider how to stir up one another to love and good works, not neglecting to meet, as is the habit of some, but encouraging one another, and all the more as you see the Day drawing near."

Hebrews 10:24-25

Michael Jordan once said, "Talent wins games, but teamwork and intelligence wins championships." Just think about that for a moment. He was really speaking of highly executed collaboration. Luke chapter 5, verse 7 tells us, "When they had done so, they caught such a large number of fish that their nets began to break. So, they signaled to their partners in the other boat to come and help them. And they came and filled both boats so full that they began to sink."

When we understand the spirit of collaboration, we all win. It is in this spirit that we understand our strengths and weaknesses. In this story, Peter is with Jesus, and they fished all night. A prior discussion had gone on, and Jesus was telling Peter to let down his nets on the right side of the boat. Peter says, "I'll let down my net." In doing so, he encountered a large group of fish. It was daytime, but what

27

is interesting is that his partners were on the shore washing their nets because they had fished all night, and their boats were out of the water. When you collaborate and understand the spirit of partnership, you know that if we win, we win together, and if we lose, we lose together. We are in a place where we are sharing good and bad. We understand resources - yours and mine. We are in this together, and we are working to benefit both groups of people.

May I suggest that in the power of collaboration, everybody does not need to win. We just need you to win because there is so much in your win. There is enough for everyone that partners with you. We do not see Peter holding back. "Well, I'll keep this net full for myself and y'all just get whatever's left over." No, no, no, no, no, no. He immediately called them over because he could not handle any more fish. His boat was full, and the net was going to break. Collaboration: he was willing to share the experience. Peter was blessed, but because he could not handle all the blessing, he had to share so that it would not go to waste. Collaborative partners bring the power of winning together. One night, Elijah and Elisha were at a campsite. An old man and young boy were preparing to go to a particular village. The army of the village had heard that Elijah and Elisha were camping out in the hills. They sent an army to surround the old man and the young boy, and they were going to attack them. Elijah had gone out the earlier part of the night at sunset and had seen the army.

The old man went back in the tent, saying nothing. The young boy went out and said, "Master, listen. There is an army getting ready to attack us." Elijah did not fear nor fret. He was not worried about it. The young boy, repeated, "Did you hear what I said?" The old man said to him, "There is more for us than against us." The story is told that the young boy does not understand what he was saying. He just did not get it. The Bible is recorded to say that Elijah says to God, "God, open his eyes." See, when you are collaborating with people, sometimes you must pray for your partners to be on the same page. You must pray so that they can see what you see. You can see the builder. You can see the customer increase. You can see the sales going through the roof. You can see bringing on new staff. You can see those things. However, your partner may not be able to see it. So, you are going to have to pray to God that your partner can see what you see. Though we are going to share in the celebration, we also must learn how to pray for those who cannot see like we do. The older man had to pray for the young boy, and the Bible says, "And when the Lord opened Elijah's eyes, he saw chariots of angels of fire and swords drawn." Because he could see-- he was a partner with Elijah. But he could not see what Elijah saw. So, if we are going to partner, we must go in the right direction. You cannot go left if I am going right. A collaborative partnership must go in the same direction. We must agree and on the same page.

Remember, talent wins championships, but teams--

wins games, but teamwork and intelligence wins championships. You must be intelligent and able to execute. I have to be able to trust that you can handle the pick and roll. I must trust you to block out. I must trust that if you are down there and do not have the shot, you will kick it back out and let somebody else take the shot. You always must operate at that level, otherwise, it will not work. You must know your position and how the game is played. You must understand that you cannot be the superstar. That may not be your assignment. Whatever role are you going to play? What value are you bringing to the table?

Where will everyone else sit if you are taking up all the space? If you are going to do it all...be the baker, the purchasing department, handle social media and public relations... what everybody else do? We never see Jesus trying to do it all. The first thing that we discovered about Jesus was that he found twelve men. He was looking for partnership. He was looking for collaborative relationships because he knew he could not get it all done. When collaborating and building relationships, you must be intelligent. You cannot be afraid to enlist the help of those who are smarter than you. I encourage you to do so. I am so encouraged when people around me are super smart, and I become enthused by their intelligence. I am rather intrigued by their intelligence. I can pick up the phone, and say, "Can you answer this question? Can you figure this out for me? What do you think about this? How do you feel about this? What are your thoughts about this time next year? How do you see that thing?" See, there is nothing wrong with people being smarter than you, but you must be confident in your own skin. You must know that you are a champion, and you cannot be defeated.

My friend, my brother, a Bishop always says, "We're better together." For years, I heard the statement, "Teamwork makes the dream work." You must know that if you are a part of a team, you cannot play all the positions. You can only play your position. If you are going to collaborate, you cannot unplug from people. You must be in your space, in your now, all the time, sharpening your skill set. If you are going to be a communicator, you must practice communication. If you are going to be a doctor, you must be around doctors. If you are a lawyer, you must be around lawyers. If you want to be a great mechanic, you are going to have to be around somebody that has a mechanical mindset. I am not saying that you cannot be around other people. However, if you are going to be great in your position, you must be around like-minded people. When Jesus wanted disciples, he wanted fishers of men. He told them, "I am going to make you fishers of man." That is how it is done. You must glean from others and create collaborative efforts to make things work. It does not mean that you are going to always agree. You will have to see it another way, and that is done through partnerships. We do that through debating and understanding how people work, how like-minded people come up with differences of opinion. I can travel to my house in Detroit in several different ways. That does not mean that your way is the right way. It just means you chose your way; I will choose mine, and we will get there at the same time. Now, does that mean I want to spend two hours extra trying to get to Detroit when you can get there an hour quicker? I do not want to spend two hours, so will listen to your direction. We are partners. We are collaborating. We are working together. We truly are better together.

Reflection Time

1. Who have you collaborated with to achieve your business goals?

2. What steps can I take to build community in my life?

The Wisdom of Stewardship

"If God was the Owner, I was the manager. I needed to adopt a steward's mentality toward the assets He had entrusted – Not Given – to me. A steward manager's assets for the Owner's benefit. The steward carries no sense of entitlement to the assets he manages. It's his job to find out what the owner wants done with His assets, then carry out His will."

— Randy Alcorn

Stewardship is the utilization and management of resources that are owned by or provided by someone else. It is important in life and business to understand the source of your ability to succeed and the resources you have been provided to do so come from God. In the most basic understanding of a resource, we have been given life, breath, and the ability to learn. We can adapt to our circumstances and grow ourselves and/or something else. You reading this book is representative of your desire to become more and grow. We are blessed with some combination of intelligence, hustle, energy, strength, skill, and other resources. All these resources are given to us by God. Some of these resources you have had for as long as you remember being alive and others you can remember developing or growing. To be clear, you are a steward over all these things. There is a responsibility and accountability to do the best that you can with what you have been given.

When you decide to create a business, you have decided to use and manage the resources and opportunities you have been given to produce something. Most of the time our businesses begin with an idea. Sometimes God will allow you to be able to see an opportunity that no one else sees. Then we have to decide whether we have the resources to support the development of that idea into a business. We have to decide whether we believe in the opportunity. Has it been provided by God? Do I have the heart, mind and energy to pursue the opportunity and bring it to fruition?

The twelve men who were sent to spy out Canaan were in the position here what God had said and believe Him more that themselves (Numbers 13:1-3). There specific instruction was to spy out the land of Canaan (opportunity) that God was going to give them. Just like the entrepreneurial and business world, they were to take the steps of any good businessperson and scout the area (Numbers 13:17-20). Observe whether the area of opportunity has strong or weak competitors and the number. Decide whether the opportunity is good or bad. Find examples to show the fruit that can be derived from the opportunity.

The twelve spies followed this same process. They were given an idea by God. I say idea, because it must be accepted or believed to be an opportunity. I believe any idea that you know has been provided by God is automatically an opportunity. Two of the spies would have agreed with me and ten would not. Even though they saw that the land was good and had great fruit (opportunity), ten of them lied. They feared the people in these lands and did not believe in God's process to give it to them like He said He would. However, two of the spies, Joshua and Caleb, accepted God's Word for what it was. His Word was a promise, an opportunity, and a resource. Joshua and Caleb understood they were stewards' His promise. They were ready to go up and take what God had given them regardless of the obstacles which lay ahead (Numbers 13:30).

When we have opportunities available, there will almost always be obstacles. Many times, the biggest obstacle to moving on the opportunities that have been presented to us is us. We don't believe in us. As the other ten spies said, "There we saw the giants (the descendants of Anak came from the giants); and we were like grasshoppers in our own sight, and so we were in their sight" (Numbers 13:33). We must decide whether we have been given stewardship over a failure. Did God give us what we need to be successful? Did God give us what we need to be good stewards? The answer is Yes. He has given us the ability to see and receive ideas/opportunities.

He has given us the ability to evaluate or scope out these opportunities. And, he has put in us the resources needed to be successful. Stewardship extends to believing what God has said. If He has given you direction, an instruction, or a promise, then you have a responsibility to extend past your belief in yourself into belief in Him.

There is an expectation that we will take what God has blessed with and grow it into more. In Matthew 25, Jesus relays to us the parable of the talents to help us understand the way things work in heaven.

> *[14] "For the kingdom of heaven is like a man traveling to a far country, who called his own servants and delivered his goods to them. [15] And to one he gave five talents, to another two, and to another one, to each according to his own ability; and immediately he went on a journey. [16] Then he who had received the five talents went and traded with them and made another five talents. [17] And likewise he who had received two gained two more also. [18] But he who had received one went and dug in the ground and hid his lord's money. [19] After a long time the lord of those servants came and settled accounts with them. (Matthew 25:14-19)*

The first thing to notice in this parable is that all the talents belong to their lord. Second like us, the servants have been given authority over the talents that were given to each of them. The first servant traded and doubled the number of talents he had. Trading involves the evaluation of assets and making good deals to increase assets. The second servant somehow doubled the money he had as well. The interesting thing I took from the second servant was that it didn't matter how it was done as long as there was increase. The last servant took his ideas, resources and opportunities and buried them where they could not benefit anyone. When their lord came back, he evaluated the work of each of his servants.

> [20] "So he who had received five talents came and brought five other talents, saying, 'Lord, you delivered to me five talents; look, I have gained five more talents besides them.' [21] His lord said to him, 'Well done, good and faithful servant; you were faithful over a few things, I will make you ruler over many things. Enter into the joy of your lord.' [22] He also who had received two talents came and said, 'Lord, you delivered to me two talents; look, I have gained two more talents besides them.' [23] His lord said to him, 'Well done, good and faithful servant; you have been faithful over a few things, I will make you ruler over many things. Enter into the joy of your lord.' (Matthew 25:20-23)

The first two servants were easy to evaluate. They did not look at what each other were doing. They were not concerned with the resources the other had received. They were concerned with gaining more for their lord. His response to both servants was the same, "Well done, good and faithful servant; you have been faithful over a few things, I will make you ruler over many things. Enter into the joy of your lord." He appreciated what they had done. He verbally acknowledged their accomplishments. He increased the area of their dominion and they entered his joy. Their experience was different than the servant who was given one talent.

> [24] *"Then he who had received the one talent came and said, 'Lord, I knew you to be a hard man, reaping where you have not sown, and gathering where you have not scattered seed.* [25] *And I was afraid and went and hid your talent in the ground. Look, there you have what is yours.'* [26] *"But his lord answered and said to him, 'You wicked and lazy servant, you knew that I reap where I have not sown, and gather where I have not scattered seed.* [27] *So you ought to have deposited my money with the bankers, and at my coming I would have received back my own with interest.* [28] *So take the talent from him and give it to him who has ten talents. (Matthew 25:20-23)*

The last servant was given one talent that he buried. He did not understand his lord or his responsibilities as a steward. A steward is not only supposed to know where resources are. A steward or good servant seeks to bring benefit not just protect. The last servant was lazy and confused. The servant was not only condemned, he also had his opportunity taken from him and was cast out.

As entrepreneurs in the wisdom of stewardship, we have a responsibility to take account of the resources we have been given – both internally and externally. We have a responsibility to scope the area we want to have our business in and the potential for success. We have a need to engage God in prayer at every step. And, we cannot allow obstacles to stop us from achieving our business goals. If we are focused on leveraging our resources for our Lord extending through to our families, we will be successful.

Reflection Time

1. What do you see as your talents in business/ personal life?

2. How can you use the resources you have been given more effectively?

The Wisdom of Preparation

"I believe success is preparation, because opportunity is going to knock on your door sooner or later, but are you prepared to answer that?"

— Omar Epps

On Jill Scott's album entitled Woman, there is a song there called Prepared. In the first verse she says, "Been letting' some old ideas go, I'm making room for my life to grow, I just wanna be prepared, yeah".

I know for some of you that would probably set you back a moment that the preacher is listening to Jill Scott. The truth is that I like Jill Scott and her music. What she does and says inspires, uplifts, encourages, and embraces life. I find her to be thought-provoking. Jill understands that in order for change and growth to occur, we must let go of some of the old. Before a step is made and decision has to take place. In the song Prepared, Jill is preparing herself for something good, something marvelous and miraculous to happen. She is preparing for the next phase of life to meet Mr. Right or the next great thing is going to happen. In order for us to receive from God it takes, us preparing us and us preparing that around us.

There are two parts of preparation. The first part is an

internal process of readying or being made ready for use or consideration. The second part is an external process of planning and getting an environment ready for an event. Both of these processes are necessary to have a healthy and thriving business. These processes need each other. We need internal and external health to be successful in business. You can have all the success you desire externally, but if you do not prepare yourself internally you can stress yourself and others out. And if you do not prepare externally by planning, you can be happy and stress free, but unable to execute effectively because you do not have a good plan.

Get Yourself Ready

Almost all of us think that we are ready for success in business without the thought of internal preparation for taking the first step. Internal preparation for success in any endeavor including business involves some basic things: prayer, obedience, and focus. These things are important, because we seek to be on the same page as God. He has visibility that we don't. He has the ability to create opportunities that we don't have access to without Him. And most importantly, we seek to please Him in every area of our lives.

Let's be clear. You are one person. You are not Joe Ordinary the Christian and Joe Ordinary the businessman. You are not Jane Simple the owner and Jane Simple the

Christian. Being a Christian should be a part of your entire life including business. God understands who you are, what you need, and desires to give it to you. "Before you were formed in the womb, I knew you" (Jeremiah 1:5). "...for your Father knows what you need before you ask Him" (Matthew 6:8).

In Isaiah 54, the Lord gives Isaiah a word for Zion's future. At the time Zion is barren, but He is telling them to have expectation. To prepare for God, they must accept His word. Before the growth takes place and the blessing arrives, they must believe and take steps. As God leads you in your business, there will be times you need to take steps based upon his direction before you see anything.

> *2 "Enlarge the place of your tent,*
> *stretch your tent curtains wide,*
> *do not hold back;*
> *lengthen your cords,*
> *strengthen your stakes.*

> *3 For you will spread out to the right and to the left;*
> *your descendants will dispossess nations*
> *and settle in their desolate cities.*

> *4 "Do not be afraid; you will not be put to shame.*
> *Do not fear disgrace; you will not be humiliated.*
> *You will forget the shame of your youth*
> *and remember no more the reproach of your*

widowhood. (Isaiah 54:2-4)

There will be some easy times and some hard times as you walk this journey, but God will be with you. Your relationship with Him is the most important aspect of your business. And, there is nothing but success that follows His footsteps.

Preparation aligning with Faith

In 2 Kings 4:1-7, there is a story of a widow who had a financial need and she asked Elisha the prophet of God for help. She had limited physical resources, but her husband had a heart after God, and she had faith in Him. God honored her faith through Elisha. She owed money to creditors that were going to take her sons into slavery to pay the debt. The first thing that she does is not written. She has hope. She hopes that once she makes Elisha aware of the situation that he will help. After she tells him of the situation, he asks her what she wants him to do and asks her what she has. Notice, he did not tell her that she had to have something particular. God is able to work with what you have. God is able to work with who you are as long as you are serving Him.

> *[1] A certain woman of the wives of the sons of the prophets cried out to Elisha, saying, "Your servant my husband is dead, and you know that your servant feared the Lord. And the creditor is coming to take my two sons to be his slaves."[2] So Elisha*

said to her, "What shall I do for you? Tell me, what do you have in the house?" And she said, "Your maidservant has nothing in the house but a jar of oil." (2 Kings 4:1-2)

The widow only has a jar of oil. She does not have seeds, but she has a seed. We would look at a jar of oil and think that there is nothing there to grow. However, God does not see the same way that we see. He sees us. He does not need the same things we need to make something grow. Your blessing may not look the way you expected it to look, but it will likely be greater than you can imagine. He needs a willing heart that will serve Him. In your business, it is easy to get caught up in what you have and don't have. Don't limit God. Get your heart and mind right and go before Him. Ask for His guidance, His direction, and His blessing. Operate in the opportunities He shows you.

After showing Elisha the jar of oil, the widow is instructed to go and borrow all of the empty vessels she can find from everywhere and he specifically said, "do not gather just a few". Do you know what she did not do? She did not question why. She did not express doubt. She listened to the instruction and was obedient.

Next, she was instructed to close the door behind her and her sons. Why? Because everyone does not always need to see how God does what he does. You don't need onlookers, doubters and questioners. Your focus is on the instruction you have been given and executing it. She then poured the oil and filled all of the vessels. And when there were no more vessels, the oil stopped. The interesting thing here is that after all of these vessels were filled, she did not then decide what to do herself. She wanted to ensure that she had the correct instruction, so she went back to Elisha and told him. Then, she was told to sell the oil, pay off her debt and live on the rest.

> *3 Then he said, "Go, borrow vessels from everywhere, from all your neighbors—empty vessels; do not gather just a few. 4 And when you have come in, you shall shut the door behind you and your sons; then pour it into all those vessels, and set aside the full ones." 5 So she went from him and shut the door behind her and her sons, who brought the vessels to her; and she poured it out. 6 Now it came to pass, when the vessels were full, that she said to her son, "Bring me another vessel." And he said to her, "There is not another vessel." So, the oil ceased. 7 Then she came and told the man of God. And he said, "Go, sell the oil and pay your debt; and you and your sons live on the rest." (2 Kings 4:1-2)*

If I were to ask what the most significant thing about this story is, many of you would say it was the miracle. If I was to ask how it happened, many would say Elisha performed the miracle. I would tell you, the most significant this happened before the happening. The widow had hope. The widow had heart. The widow had focus. The widow knew she needed God and hoped He would answer. He did.

Have a plan

Alan Lakein says that planning is bringing the future into the present so that we can do something about it. What we want to do about it is strategize, examine, and figure out the best way. Planning and preparation do not ensure success but provide a roadmap. Now I must admit, this is not my strong suit as a leader. Though I like strategizing and planning, I am not the biggest proponent of writing things down. This is where team members come into play. I am grateful to the people that work with me. They are great at what they do. We can tweak and adjust where needed.

This type of collaboration will not happen just because you say so. Nor will it happen just because you have a plan. You are going to have to take some initiative and adjust. Some sacrifices are going to have to be made. Remember, plans work by bringing them from your present into your future so you can do something about it. What are you going to do about it? Now that you know what you want to do, now that you know how much the house is going to cost, now that you know how much square footage you are going to need, now that you know how much product you are going to have to have, what are you going to do about it? What are you going to put together to make this work? How are you going to obtain the down payment for the new kitchen? How are you going to develop people? What processes will you use to train others so that they do not burn the place down? What happens if the place catches on fire? Does anybody know how to get to a fire extinguisher? Is there an exit strategy? Does anybody know where the exits are located? Does anybody know who to call if you are unavailable? Planning is crucial. Planning is necessary.

At least once a year in our congregation, we have a strategic planning session about fire safety. We must plan how to evacuate the building in an emergency. We are also planning other things that go on in our congregation, such as maintenance and a couple other things that need to happen. Strategically, someone must sit down and think about what it takes to move this group of people out of the building.

Currently, we are planning for a large event within the next couple of months. What do we do? What time will the speakers arrive? What time will the entertainment arrive? What time will they leave the hotel? How long does it take them to travel from the hotel to the church? How long does it take them to get from the airport to the hotel? Timing is everything and is a crucial part of planning. Therefore, you must know what you do not know, and you must ask questions. There are no dumb questions. The only bad question is the one that is not asked. As leaders, we must encourage people to ask questions. They need to know the details, how things are going to work, and how they will work so that no one is left in the dark. Poor execution makes for a poor program.

Leaders must be able to execute at a much higher level than most people. You must know that your team will execute. Recently in a team meeting, the following statement was made, "Pastor, you only have a short window. You only have about 3 months." Typically, it takes about six months, if not longer, to really plan something out. After all, you do not want to just throw something together. You want to make sure you have the right people doing the right things. So, yes, it takes some time to plan things. I know some people may say, "Oh, it does not take all of that." Well, let me help you. Some people are on different levels. My level may be a little bit because of my capacity. However, planning, at any level, is necessary. I have been on both ends of the spectrum. Truthfully, I have been all over the spectrum at this point. I have been in the storefronts and in a house. We have grown from 75 people to a sizeable number every Sunday: packed, enjoying worship, buying property, and canceling debt. God has really been good and kind to me, but it took planning.

The first church that I pastored, we decided we wanted to be out of debt. We committed to a strategic plan and were able to do that. We said, "This is what we want to do. This is the money we are going to raise. We are going to take a piece every week and put it aside. We will pay towards the principal." When we started doing that, before we knew it, God's favor was on us and we were out of debt. We then went from being out of debt to buying a significant piece of land to develop. I am grateful to God for the experience. If He has done it once, then He can do it again, but it takes planning. It takes people being on the same page. Now, I am in another ministry, doing well. We are coming into another out-of-debt scenario. I see it coming. I envision it. We have a plan that we are executing to make that happen, because it takes vision. The Bible says, "Where there is no vision, the people perish." So, you must have a plan. You must have partners at the table.

I remember some time ago listening to Bishop I.V. Hilliard comment that he often converses with his family about vision for the church and his family. He would allow them to scrutinize his vision and his plans to expose any holes. I find this an interesting thing to do because we do not often hear our leaders giving people permission to scrutinize what they believe. Often as leaders, we just do it, but sometimes we need to know if it is doable. I know guys and girls who jumped into building programs and sank the church because no one questioned them. No one said, "Is this really what we should be doing right now?" We are not saying do not do it, but could we get ten more members? We have five now and you are talking about a half million dollar building project. So, we want to make sure it lines up. We want to make sure that God is in the planning and the process, and then He will make provision.

He makes it doable for all of us. He gives us proper perspective on everything. We want to examine closely to ensure that plans are adequate. Do we have supplies? Do we have God's permission? This is critical. I have been in predicaments where God has said to me, "Wait." I am in a holding pattern right now about something that I want to do. God is saying, "Wait." Have you ever heard God say, "Wait?" In the end, the question is, do you wait, or do you proceed? More times than not, honestly, I proceeded. Surely God would not have given me this vision to tell me to wait? The Scripture tells us "wait on the Lord," and "be of good courage, and He shall renew thy heart," and strengthen you. You do not know what is ahead of you.

He may have given you the vision, but He also may tell you to wait at this junction because the economy is going to shift. People are going to lose their jobs in your area, and then you are going to be out. I remember so vividly, a friend of mine who has gone to be with the Lord, calling me, all excited about a building project that he had embarked upon. Man, that thing turned out to be a nightmare for him; a complete nightmare. If I remember correctly, it took almost ten plus years to build this project. Banks had levied on the building, and contractors went to jail. It was horrible. Just because you have the vision does not mean you have the green light to implement it.

I have been on both ends of that, and I am not saying I am perfect by any means. There were times when God has told me to wait on something. I went ahead and did it, and

I pay for it. Let me tell you, I have paid severely for missing God. Money, good people, time, energy, effort, and I have spent a lot of time trying to compensate for my mess ups. So, I want to encourage you to seek God's permission, even when you have a plan.

The Bible says that there is safety in the multitude of counsel. Take some time to examine your counsel. If you have never been on a building project, and you do not have a person who knows what building is like, and you don't have anyone that you can lean on, you will be lost. I am referring to building anything… a relationship, a house, church, etc. You need people that will tell you the truth. Do not put people in positions where they have no expertise. You would not place a plumber in charge of electricians. You are setting yourself up for failure. You are setting your project up for failure. Your name will be scandalized. You must live after that project is over. If you are opening a business, you must know you have wherewithal. Did you get the best deal? Did you get three bids? Sometimes it requires four. You must ensure success, safety, and a reputable installation so that you know you got the best bang for your buck. Nothing is just going to happen. You must plan and plan again.

We are currently wrapping up a four-year project worth millions of dollars. This is the first project that we have done of this large amount. Time and people have made me prove that I know what I am doing. I am okay with that because neither the race nor the battle is given to the swift nor the strong but to the one that endures until the very end.

We need to have integrity and the right motive. We really need to know that we have the green light from God to make this thing work. So, I want to encourage you: plan, plan, and plan some more. Take those plans to somebody else. Say, "What do you think about them? Do you see anything that we could be doing differently?" Have you opened a store or a boutique? Do you have your EIN number? Do you have your articles of incorporation? Do you have the right documentation? Are you ready for taxes; local, state, and federal? What is required? These questions come with planning and execution. Do you have an attorney? You may say, "I do not need an attorney. It is just me." Listen, you need somebody that can represent you if someone walks in your shop and slips and falls? Do you have proper and adequate insurance? Are you underinsured? Planning erases these questions. Counsel alleviates them. I encourage you, as you begin to plot your plan, whether as a developing individual or in a corporate or small business setting, plan, plan, plan. You cannot go wrong when you have a plan.

Reflection Time

1. How do you need to prepare yourself?

2. What steps do you need to take to build a plan?

The Wisdom of Failure

*"If "Plan A" does not work, the alphabet
has 25 more letters."*

— Author Unknown

Failure has been a part of my everyday life in regard to
wanting to be in business. To be honest, if you are going
to be an entrepreneur, failure will be part of your DNA. I
know our culture does not teach us to respect or appreciate
failure. The truth is that failure is going to be a part of your
life. It is going to be woven into your DNA, the very fiber
and core of who you are. Without failure, there will be no
appreciation for success, and one must begin now to
understand and appreciate the lessons that failure brings all
of us.

Honestly, failure is not pleasant, but one can learn to
appreciate it. Failure comes to teach you what nothing else
can. It has a class, and your name is on the roster. You will
begin to understand failure when you can embrace the
teachable moments that it brings to each one of our lives.
Failure breeds some of the most beautiful things in life. It
is failure that allows and motivates me to get up every day
after being told, "No," from a bank. It is failure that allows
me to go back and rewrite my business plan, understand
my plot in life, how things are going to work, who is for
me and who is not. A lot of us want to have the

cheerleaders in our room and office. However, as an entrepreneur, let me explain something.

Failure is going to be your best friend. When you do not get the loan or the right employees, when things just do not go right, failure will keep you focused on what truly you should be doing. It is failure that enables you to see what you cannot see on a sunny day. Failure allows us to know and understand the hurts and triumphs of life and how then to appreciate those moments of success. You cannot give up now. You have too much at stake. There are people in your community, your church, and even your neighborhood who need you. Failure will expose the greater parts of you. You will learn what you can endure. You will learn how to make the bills work out. When someone does not show up for work, you will learn how to do it all. You will understand how to open and close. You will understand what it is like to do the things that are necessary to learn, and the baby steps are your entrepreneurial journey. You do not learn these things by having millions of dollars at your disposal. You do not learn these things by always having cheerleaders around and people embracing you. You need people who will walk out of your life. You need someone who will not show up to encourage you. You need someone to dig a ditch, to throw a rock, to hide their hand. You're going to need someone to stab you in the back. These things in life create the person we long to see. In the Bible, David says, "It is the one that I gave sweet counsel to that has done me the most harm." Without it, we would not get the 23rd Psalm, or Psalm 73, or even Psalms 108. There are so many things that are revealed in us through the tragedies.

I must admit, it is not always easy. I could not tell you about failure if I have not sat at its table and learned its lessons, eating from its bitter bread, or drank its wines of sorrow. These have me to be the man that I am. It is these things that people want to hear and understand that if you can overcome that, I can trust you with this. I am so excited to announce to you that failure also promotes you over a period of time. There comes a point in life where failure will reward you for the efforts you have made. It will reward you in the form of the things needed right when you need them the most because you were willing to suffer and endure through heartache, scuffle as though no one else could see it, and would not turn the back on your dream.

Failure will teach you and promote you. When it promotes you, let me tell you, there is nothing greater than the sweetness of success. The truth is that there is absolutely no success without failure. It is the process of going through these bitter moments in our lives that causes us to be the great champions of our day. You cannot have success without failure. It is the twin that makes things work in our lives. I would like to encourage you to endure your failures. Smile with them, and cry with them, if you must. What you cannot do is give up and give out. It is not a part of who you are. Believe me, greatness is who you are. Victorious is what you are. Overcomer is who you are.

You can go back and rewrite the business plan, rewrite the grant, take one more class, hire the right person. Through it all, failure will be your friend. It will promote and pay off. Failure will cause good people to take note of you and the efforts you have put forth. But it only comes over a period of time, a period of disappointment, a period where you are not going to be able to throw in the towel.

You are going to have, what I call, a stick-to-itiveness. This is the ability to stick it out until you get what you need or desire. However, this comes at a high price. Just know failure is not all bad. It brings some amazing things in our lives if we would just learn to embrace the lessons that it wants to teach us each day. This makes life beautiful, and it gives us the value that people want to hear about. Remember, failure is coming your way. Smile and live.

Every Day is Not a Win

Let me tell you, there are going to be some days when you are not going to win. There are going to be some weeks when you will not win. You need to be prepared for this reality sooner than later. Typically, we all become discouraged with multiple losses, setbacks, or disappointments occurring in a process. It is just who we are as humans. Being prepared, looking on the horizon, and identifying are important. I am not saying that you will wake up every day wanting to win, but just know in your mind, every day is not a win. It then begins to transform your thinking to understand that you must learn from every day, regardless if it is a win or not. These wins and setbacks are all facets of teaching, and if you only want to win, you will never appreciate the process.

The moments when we are not doing well are the great moments. It is when the employee that you have hired and worked hard to train suddenly gets another job, not bothering to tell you that they are not coming in. It is when you know you have paid the bills or utilities, only to go to the shop, and the lights are not on. Someone has unfortunately broken in, or a fire has occurred. Every day is not a win in an entrepreneur's life. This journey is tough. This journey is vast. This journey is something to behold for those of us that are born to do it. This is a calling. I answered my phone and listened to the instructions that were given to me.

Oftentimes, God uses the endgame to draw us into that which He is calling us to do. So, He shows us the ending of a process before he shows us the middle so that we become intrigued to, what I call, get off the porch. Even then, disappointments are going to come. There will be a period when you will have all great days and success. Sometimes, for my lack of entertainment, I play a game called Phase 10. I started out playing it with my children. They taught me the game, the principals and how to play. As kids do, they grew up and left home. I find myself sometimes wanting to play, but they are not available. Then, I discovered the app, and now, I play regularly. The game does several things for me. It teaches me that I am not going to win every hand. I do not care how good you are, how much you strategize, or how much energy you use, you will not win every hand. I can go many days without winning, but then, there are days that I win hand after hand. Both days have me on edge because I am determined to know when the cycle will shift and see how I fair tomorrow.

As an entrepreneur, you must be agile and able to handle trends and transcending movements of markets. Everybody is not buying blue this week. If you have a ton of blue in your shop, how do you sell it? You create a trend, a movement, a wave, buzz. You have the power to make changes. When things shift, you can shift with them, turning negatives into positives. The power lies within you as an entrepreneur. You can sit there, cry, and get no bills paid that day. You can go home and close the shop early. You could tell everybody in the nail shop, dress shop, or plant, "Go home, I am having a difficult day," or you can keep playing the game. You can keep playing the hand that has been dealt to you. Knowing that you are not going to win today does not mean you do not come back to play tomorrow. You have to know without a doubt that you are in this to win.

You have to believe in yourself and know how things are going to go. Every day of your life may not be a win, but you *are* going to win. Can I help you with something? There will be a time where every day is a win, every day is a victory. Every time you turn around, it is going to work out. There are going to be those days. It is called life. Life happens to all of us. There are chances and opportunities that will present themselves. The benefit of chances and opportunities is that they balance themselves out. So, the employee quit but did not call you. Move on to the next one. So, somebody walked out of your life, and it hurts. It was someone that you loved. It was someone that you cared about. I get it. Pain is deep. Listen, every day is not a win, but enjoy the wins while they last. Enjoy the victories while they come. Enjoy the mountaintop experiences while they happen. Just know, the same way that life took you up, there are going to be some down times. There are going to be some twists. There are going to be some turns.

I used to take my kids to Disney World, and for the most part, they had good experiences. My wife and I tried to give them a balanced, well-rounded life. The thing about Disney World is, there are roller coasters everywhere. You know what I have discovered about all of them? They all have something in common. They start, and they stop. That roller coaster has a starting point and an ending point. What is interesting is that, most times, the starting point and ending points are the same. Often, where you start and where you end are the same. The difference is that you enter in on one side of the coaster and exit on the other. A roller coaster is a circle with twists and turns. People pay good money to get on roller coasters to be scared out of their mind and get sick. Yet, we complain about the roller coaster that life puts us on, as though we were not expecting it.

We complain about people walking out. That is just the loop. We complain about people lying on us. That is a dip. We complain about not being treated right. That is a twist. We complain about people misusing us. That is a turn. It is a roller coaster. Can I help you with something else? Just like the roller coasters at an amusement park, people get in one way and get off a whole other way. In life, it is the same process. People come in one way: Oh, I am a fan. I am going to get it. I am with you. I am down for whatever. I am here for you, brother. Whatever I can do for you, sister. I am here. You discover that when the ride gets too hard and the days get too long, they are like anybody else. They want off this coaster. God, I do not understand what happened, but let me help you. You cannot expect people to ride with you when they did not pay to get on in the first place. You must pay to ride with me because I cannot trust you if you do not pay the fare. I have to be able to know that you are here. If we are going to win, we win together. If we are going to lose, we lose together. Now, please understand. I said it in other chapters, and I want to reiterate it now. You have to know the difference in corner people and circle people. You must know who is in your corner versus who is in your circle. Please, sir. Please, ma'am. Take the time out and discover who is in your corner versus who is in your circle.

Disappointments

John 16:33. Good news translation. I have told you this so that you will have peace, by being united to me. The world will make you suffer but be brave. I have defeated the world.

I would like to discuss disappointments and trouble. Disappointments and trouble are scheduled. As we take close examination of our lives, we will truly discover and understand that there are some things that have gone on in our lives that are scheduled to happen. It is scheduled for us to have trouble. It is scheduled for us to be disappointed. It is a fact of life. None of us, whether we are rich or poor, will ever be able to go around this issue of trouble and disappointments. No matter how much money you have or how little money you have, troubles are going to come. It does not matter if you stay in the most influential neighborhood or most impoverished one, trouble is going to come.

Disappointments is the twin of trouble. They normally run together. It is important to understand that trouble and disappointment are just part of the fiber of life. As these things come, they are not coming to discourage us. They are not coming to railroad us. They are not coming to disconnect us. Rather, they come to strengthen us and enable us to see life through a whole other lens. I do not know how many times we have had this discussion with groups of people, but we tell them that it is the way you look at it. It is the way you see it. It is how you envision it. Is the glass half empty, or is it half full? Are you going to be a victim or victorious? Are you going to lay in the defeat and tell about who would not help you and who did not like you? On the contrary, are you going to raise up, dust yourself off, and encourage and speak words of empowerment to yourself so that you can overcome every obstacle that comes your way? It is David, and Ziklag is where we look and find him. His family has been taken prisoner by the Philistines - his wives and children, along with all the mighty men. David has been out on a campaign, and when he returns to Ziklag, he has discovered that the city has been burned and the families of all his mighty men have been taken prisoner. Scripture says that these men, who once cheered him on and encouraged him "turned on him," and now, they are ready to stone him for what has gone on to their families.

It will be the people that sing your praises that will turn on you. The Bible says that David called to the priest and told him to bring the ether. He would adorn himself with the ether and began to seek the face of God. David asked God, "Should I pursue, and will I overtake them?"

Before you launch your business, start your next venture, or step out on another platform, will you ask God, "Am I going to be successful? Is this what you are saying to me? Do I have enough stamina to endure? Will I be victorious? Do I have with me all that is needed to prevail?" Being an entrepreneur, a husband, a wife, just living in general, none of us want to lose. All of us want to win.

Winning is part of what we want and part of our makeup. You can only win if you invoke the winner on your side. He is on your side, but you must engage Him, and you must tell him that you need him to win. You do not want to just win, but you want to be victorious. You want to overcome every obstacle. David, in this case, understood that the families had been taken prisoner. His children and wives all are gone. The enemy had them. What is interesting is that as he invokes the presence of God, prays and talks to God about the scenario and the situation, he feels the pressure of the 600 men. Not only has David's family been taken prisoner, but the 600 mighty men that were with him were taken prisoner. They are astonished and hurt that their families are gone. The camp has been vandalized and burned to the ground. So, David is inquiring God, "Can I, will I, shall I overtake them? Can I be victorious? Can I beat them, and will I overtake them and bring back the spoils? Will I bring back what is rightfully mine? Someone is probably thinking, "Well, this business is not mine. This shop is not mine." I hasten to tell you that it is. The very reason that you have a dream for it is because it is rightfully yours. The very reason that you have a desire to open it is because it is rightfully yours. The ability to conceptualize and envision a finished product says that it is yours. You cannot envision anything that God has not already given you to be yours. The envision of the item says that it is on God's mind for you to possess it. However, can you put the plan together to obtain what God has rightfully given you? The business is yours. It is yours to be successful, but is there a plan?

Disappointments, tragedies and troubles are scheduled. These things are going to happen. The missing element that helps us overcome them is putting a plan in place. Stick to your plan. Write that vision. Make it plain. Do this in preparation for when trouble comes, and you cannot envision anymore. Things will happen to clog our vision and thinking, and to prevent us from moving forward. It is going to happen, and that is okay. Do not panic. When we cannot see anymore, when we are no longer able to envision the vision, then we must rely on what was envisioned the first time.

See things from a new perspective. February is Black History Month. One day in February, as I was listening to the radio, I heard the movie Black Panther was reshowing in theaters. It is interesting that the producers and the theater owners were playing the movie for free. Why would they do this during Black History Month? This is one of the rarest times, or perhaps the first time that all cast members, all the rated cast members, all the top cast members, the production, the whole gamut of a movie is Black. I did a little research on the movie Black Panther and discovered that the entire movie was filmed at Tyler Perry's studio in Atlanta. So, not only do you have Black cast, but the set that you shoot it on was owned by a Black man.

Now, please hear me out. I am not about to debate race or racial issues. That is not what we are here for. I am here to encourage people because so many times in the African American community, we do not get to see this level of Blackness. We have not seen it at this level, and we want to celebrate it. We want to embrace these moments that we are now raising up to be our own storytellers, directors, and cast members to tell our story that way that we see it from our own lens. I thank God for all the other movies that have come out and particularly have had black people in them. I thank God for all of them. However, in this particular one, we are celebrating the fact that everything about Black Panther is Black, and we are excited.

Now, let me get back to David. David knows now that God has given him permission. Remember ownership. Ownership is what David is after because the things that he has owned have been taken from him. So, when you envision starting a business, a bakery, a grocery store, a hair salon, beauty salon, barber shop, or becoming a massage therapist, psychologist, doctor, dentist, playwright, movie studio owner, etc., it is yours. God has given you the ability not only to envision it but to possess it. Trouble brings this about. See, there would have been no need for David to approach God had his family not been taken. When trouble is scheduled, it brings something out in us that peace does not. Trouble does what sunny days do not do for us. When trouble comes, we raise the game. We raise the level of intensity. We raise the ability to see farther than we have ever seen before. So, of course, the story goes that David and the 600 men are pursuing vigorously. They are running. They are moving at a rapid pace. They are moving at such a rapid pace that David must leave half of his troops at the river because they cannot keep up with him. Let me share something with you. As an entrepreneur, everybody will not to be able to keep up with you. Now, remember, the story does not end there. As the story proceeds, David finds a young lad that had been left for dead. Someone else had discarded him as being insignificant, no longer having value, no longer being worth anything, no ability to add any value. Since you are of no value to me, I will leave you in this field to die. The young boy makes a deal with David. He says, "I will show you where my master is under the conditions that you do not kill me, and that you do not turn me back over to my master." David agrees to this. Now I want to share with you that along the way, you must learn that everybody is not your enemy. Had David killed the boy, he never would have seen the value in what the boy had to offer. You must know when people have been placed in your path for purpose to get you somewhere a lot quicker than normal. David was at a divided road at this place and needed to know which way they went. He was uncertain, given the geographical layout. Sometimes, to not go down the wrong road, you must listen to someone whom you think could possibly be your enemy tell you which way you need to go.

Listen to what I am saying because this is a very, very sticky scenario. This young boy was truly a part of the enemy's camp, but the boy himself was not an enemy of David. He was a part of them by slavery. Some people that you will encounter may be with your enemies as you see it externally. However, you will have to examine closely to determine if the person that you are going to embrace is for information or relationship. The second thing you need to do is evaluate the people that you have found along the way. Just because they ran with your enemy does not make them your enemy. You do not know what the scenario that they were in while they were with your enemy. If they are willing to help you, why not listen to them? So, the young boy tells David how to find his master. David immediately gets the rest of the men and follows the boy. This has cut time out of David's chase, perhaps days. Could the person that you are getting ready to meet cut years out of your process? They are worth examining. They are worth hearing out. They are worth examining. When David discovered where they were, the Bible says he went in immediately and engaged in battle. He fought them from sun-up to sun-down. Many men got away on camels, but most were killed.

I am telling you, that your dream is worth the fight. If God has given you a vision, he has also given you provision. If your vision and your provision are in the enemy's camp, you need to take your stuff back. You need to seek God for a strategic plan on how to get your stuff back. If you have permission, promise, and passion, you have victory. You need permission from God, passion for the thing that you are going after, and be in pursuit. You have absolute victory on your hands. However, it is not going to come easy. The Bible says in this story that David had to do a lot. Notice that David's victory did not just bless him but all of those that started out with him. He gathered all the spoils and people; all his family and the other men's' families. As you open your shop, you are not just in business for you. There are some other people that are going to be inspired and motivated to do what you are doing, and you want to help them. You want to assist them. David took all the spoils back. He picked up the 300 men that he left at the river, but the men that had gone with him to fight became very indignant. They told David, "Listen, we are not going to split this evenly because they did not make the trip. They did not make the journey. They did not put the work in. David, being a man of integrity and compassion, said to those men, "It is not right to take their stuff when we all have suffered loss. Give them what is rightfully due to them. It is not their fault that they could not keep up with me." There are some people that have helped you along the way. You need to be able to say thank you to them. Do not get convenient amnesia because you did not get here by yourself. You did not know how to ride to the point where you are alone. I do not care if you divorced her. I do not care if he left you. What is right to do, they suffered with you. They went through with you, and now you are at the point of receivership. You are at the point of getting and moving on and developing something great. Now you are at this point. Guess what? You are also at the point of being a blessing to someone else, and we want you to be a blessing. We do not want you to be disgruntled to the point that God permits the enemy to come back in and take what you worked long and hard to get. That is not what we want to happen.

We want to see you constantly victorious. We want to know that you are victorious, not just in the spotlight, but even when the lights are out. I want the anointing of God, the pleasure and the promise of God, to be an illuminated light in darkness. There are some people that have struggled with you, who know your heartache, struggle, and pain. All of this came by way of the struggle. Remember, in the Scripture, Jesus said, "I have overcome the world. I have defeated the world. I have taken what the world had to offer, and I made lemons for my lemonade. I have taken the heartache, and I made something good." Yes, they left you. That is nothing to be proud of, but it happened. It is over now. I have overcome the world. I have overcome the heartache. I have overcome the discouragement. I have overcome you walking out on me and telling me I will never amount to anything. I have overcome that. I am so over it that I can be good to those who hurt me. I can be good to those who mistreated me. I can be good to those who did me wrong, dug ditches, threw rocks, and said I would never make it. I have made it now.

I know trouble is scheduled. It is going to come. However, just as much as trouble comes, I have victory. I am going through with a smile. Every day is not a smile, but when you put my good days against my bad days, I have will not complain. All my good days are outweighing my bad days. I will not complain. I am getting victory on the other side of this trouble. I have an overcoming faith on the other side of this trouble. I see the light in the midst of my sorrow. It cannot rain always. David gives the men who could not make the journey their rightful portion. He did not have to do it, but the God in him said it was the right thing to do. It is the God in you. I am not saying it must be money but send them flowers to say thank you. Send them a postcard that says, "I made it." Send them a note and say, "Still here and doing well. Thank you for all you have done for me." You must be bigger than that. You must be bigger than your trouble. Remember the text says, "The world will make you suffer." Well, I choose not to suffer. I can be afflicted without suffering. I will not complain. I am going to seek the face of God so that He will give me a plan. Then, I am going to act on the plan.

Remember, there are some people that I need who ran with my enemy. Those are going to be the very people to show me where my stuff is located. When they show me where my stuff is, I will be able to gather it after the war. Nothing is going to come easy. There will be a war for you to obtain what God has envisioned you to seek. Even in that, He will give you faith, strength, and power to carry out the strategic plan. He sent you some help. Take your stuff. When you take it, take all of it? The Bible says, "He took everything back." Once you have it, please do not forget to share with those that have struggled with you along the way. Share with those people that have seen you in your rough days. Thank those people, because without them, you would not have been able to make it. Without them, you would not see what you are seeing right now. Turn that thing around on them. Remember, this too, yeah, I believe it, shall pass. You have victory like you cannot believe.

Reflection Time

1. What was your greatest failure?

2. What can you do to mitigate future failure or bounce back after failure occurs?

The Wisdom of Grit

"Grit is that extra something that separates the most successful people from the rest. It is passion, perseverance, and stamina that we must channel to stick with our dreams until they become a reality."

— Travis Bradberry

Grit is a personality trait possessed by individuals who demonstrate passion and perseverance toward a goal despite being confronted by significant obstacles and distractions. Those who possess grit can self-regulate and postpone their need for positive reinforcement while working diligently on a task.

You may be asking, what does that mean?

For years, psychologists have attempted to locate the "miracle formula" needed to achieve our dreams. Many have thought that possibly a high IQ, great achievement, a stroke of luck or maybe even fate is the answer. While none of those factors have proven to generate any kind of miracle formula, research has found evidence that possessing the quality of grit is the highest predictor of an individual achieving greatness.

Grit is "stick-to-itiveness;" a diligent spirit; the nagging conviction that keeps you pressing on when it would be easier to give up. Grit is what makes you get back on the horse after you have been kicked off. Grit is the realization that achieving one's greatest potential comes from running a marathon, not a sprint. As an entrepreneur you will need this skill or spirit to be successful. There will be failures. There will be trials and tribulations. There will be times when you just have to wait out the storm.

In a society fueled by instant gratification, possessing grit is not as simple a task as one may initially believe. One of the biggest indicators of grit is an ability to delay gratification while working on a task. Simple in theory, but very difficult in practice — especially in today's technological world. One of the reasons why social media sites like Twitter and Facebook have become so addictive is that they offer users quick, accessible bursts of positive reinforcement with likes and retweets and hearts. The second most important characteristic of grit is the ability to remain constant even though significant challenges arise along the way. These characteristic prods a little deeper into our beliefs about our own worth and self-efficacy, as well as our explanations for why challenges arise in the first place. Those with grit do not look at their difficulties or failures as a reason to quit; rather, they utilize them as opportunities to grow stronger and become better equipped for the next challenge.

How do I use this in my life?

If one wants to become excellent at anything, be it

basketball, algebra, public speaking, healthy eating, money management, organization, or even their marriage, they must commit to avoiding distractions and persevering when challenges arise. Sure, talent, intelligence, and being at the right place at the right time may all play some role in achieving success, but it is really the quality of being gritty that will prove to be most critical on your quest. There really is no way around it: working hard is necessary if you want to get what you want. The good news is that being gritty can be learned, and there are a few things we can do to teach this characteristic to ourselves:

Manage your distractions. We all have things in our life that pull us away from what really matters. Whether it is social media, television, our unhealthy habits, or an unhealthy relationship, they all offer us early rewards without lasting value. Discover what most commonly distracts you. Determine what small reward it is offering you. In your moments of temptation, remind yourself of the greater reward that you are trying to achieve in realizing your ultimate goal.

Eradicate your "fixed mindset." The results are in success does not just land itself on the laps of those who are privileged, blessed, or lucky. Talent is earned; if you desire it, you must work for it.

Confront your fears of failure. Everyone fails and encounters some level of challenge. If something is valuable enough to you, decide that you are willing to experience some amount of failure to achieve it. Without that, you will not be vulnerable enough to just begin.

Generate your own early rewards. When there's a task that feels big, it's easy to get discouraged. If you break it down into smaller pieces and reward yourself along the way, you will be more aware of your progress and more likely to stay motivated to the task at hand.

Reflection Time

1. Think of a time in your life where you used grit to get through?

2. What does a fixed mindset mean to you?

The Wisdom of the 2 R's

"This is a hard truth for some to accept: that a lack of resources may not be their true constraint, just a lack of resourcefulness."

— David Burkus

"Resilience isn't a single skill. It's a variety of skills and coping mechanisms. To bounce back from bumps in the road as well as failures, you should focus on emphasizing the positive."

— Jean Chatzky

The 2R's as I call them. Resilience and Resourcefulness. Resilience and Resourcefulness are two key characteristics necessary to be a successful entrepreneur. I remember growing up and watching the older folks on set incomes feed neighborhoods. They took a little of nothing and made it into a whole lot of something. They seemed otherworldly, because magically they took limited resources and, in some cases, created a masterpiece. This is the definition of resourcefulness; making something out of nothing. As a business owner, there will be times when you have limited resources, especially when you first start out. However, successful entrepreneurs take what little they have and find a way to multiply it. It is the difference between those who get it done and those who complain about what they don't have. Have you ever thought about how resourceful you are? If you haven't now would be an appropriate time to ask yourself what you are made of. The game of business ownership is not for those who can't figure out how to be industrious.

Potatoes, Eggs, and Coffee Beans

Once upon a time a daughter complained to her father that her life was miserable and that she didn't know how she was going to make it. She was tired of fighting and struggling all the time. It seemed just as one problem was solved, another one soon followed.

Her father, a chef, took her to the kitchen. He filled three pots with water and placed each on a high fire. Once the three pots began to boil, he placed potatoes in one pot, eggs in the second pot, and ground coffee beans in the third pot.

He then let them sit and boil, without saying a word to his daughter. The daughter, moaned and impatiently waited, wondering what he was doing.

After twenty minutes he turned off the burners. He took the potatoes out of the pot and placed them in a bowl. He pulled the boiled eggs out and placed them in a bowl.

He then ladled the coffee out and placed it in a cup.

Turning to her he asked. "Daughter, what do you see?"

"Potatoes, eggs, and coffee," she hastily replied.

"Look closer," he said, "and touch the potatoes." She did and noted that they were soft. He then asked her to take an egg and break it. After pulling off the shell, she observed the hard-boiled egg. Finally, he asked her to sip the coffee. Its rich aroma brought a smile to her face.

"Father, what does this mean?" she asked.

He then explained that the potatoes, the eggs and coffee beans had each faced the same adversity– the boiling water.

However, each one reacted differently.

The potato went in strong, hard, and unrelenting, but in boiling water, it became soft and weak.

The egg was fragile, with the thin outer shell protecting its liquid interior until it was put in the boiling water. Then the inside of the egg became hard.

However, the ground coffee beans were unique. After they were exposed to the boiling water, they changed the water and created something new.

"Which are you," he asked his daughter. "When adversity knocks on your door, how do you respond? Are you a potato, an egg, or a coffee bean? "

Which one are you? - Unknown

This story illustrates Resilience or what I call the bounce back. The question is not if you will run into problems, it is when. As I've stated before you will fail and fail again before you succeed. Your success will be directly tied to your bounce back capability. Can you rise above your circumstances and come out better on the other side or do you lay down in the face of hardship and stay there? This chapter is designed for you to think about your metal as a person and an entrepreneur. If you have a non-existent bounce back game, entrepreneurship is not for you. I don't want to discourage you from stepping into this journey, but rather engage your thinking about how you handle life when trouble comes.

In life, things happen around us, things happen to us, but the only thing that truly matters is what happens within us and how we use it.

Reflection Time

1. Who is the most resourceful person you know? How are they resourceful?

2. Who is the most resilient person you know? How are they resilient?

The Wisdom of Mindset

"Common sense would suggest that having ability, like being smart, inspires confidence. It does, but only while the going is easy. The deciding factor in life is how you handle setbacks and challenges. People with a growth mindset welcome setback with open arms."

— **Travis Bradberry**

So, let's dig a little more into mindset. I introduced the term "fixed mindset in a previous chapter and I will now cover mindset entirely. Mindset is simply an established set of attitudes a person has. It has been discovered there are two types of attitudes that fall under mindset: the fixed mindset and the growth mindset. People who have a fixed mindset believe that things such as intelligence and skills are fixed and can't be improved upon. They believe you are born with what you have and that is it. On the other hand, growth mindset people believe intelligence and skills can be improved upon and enhanced.

You may be asking yourself at this point, what does mindset have to do with anything, let alone entrepreneurship. Well success in entrepreneurship will require you to have a growth mindset. You see, people with a fixed mindset struggle to be successful. They may be that naturally athletic football player in high school or that popular cheerleader who everyone praised. Then when you see them at the 10-year class reunion, they haven't really moved in life, they are still living in their glory days and the are not trying to learn to moved forward. Somewhere along the line, they believed they hit their peak. They went to college and started competing against people with the same or elevated skills and because of their fixed mindset, they never worked to get better. In fact, they spent a huge amount of time covering for their shortcomings, blaming others and hiding their fears. Then you have your moderately athletic football player or your student who struggled academically in high school, but you see them at the 10-year class reunion and find the football player went on to play professionally and the student has received a master's degree from Yale. Mind boggling, right? But if you really think about it, it makes all the sense in the world. The people with the growth mindset continued to push themselves and continued to learn. They didn't try to hide their deficiencies, they embraced them and continued to get better. Whereas, the fixed mindset people stopped right in their tracks. Their perspective was off.

Have you ever had someone say to you, "It's all about perspective,"? That's what mindset is – the way you look at yourself, the people in your life, your business and the world around you. If you have a growth mindset, you understand that the harder you work, the more drive you have, and the more optimism you use when facing the world, the more successful you'll be. I guarantee you will need a growth mindset as an entrepreneur.

Fortunately, you can change your mindset. If you change your mindset, you can change your life.

Reflection Time

1. Take a minute to consider yourself and your perception? Are you a fixed mindset person or do you have more of a growth mindset perspective?

2. What steps can I take to be a more open-minded person?

The Wisdom of Self-Care

"Solitude is where I place my chaos to rest
and awaken my inner peace."

— Nikki Rowe

Well my friends, I thought it appropriate that I end this book looking at physical and spiritual wellbeing. In other words, let's talk about self- care. This is a touchy subject to me because like so many of us in our community and in our world, I have done what I should when it comes to spiritual and physical wellbeing. Like so many of us, I have not taken care of my physical body. I have consumed things that would come back to hurt me later in my life. I didn't know better in the past, but I get it now. Man, do I get it now because I'm paying an extremely high price. It's nobody's fault but my own. My poor eating habits, poor dieting, and little to no exercise led to less than optimal physical health. My body reminded me that there's a bill that must be paid for poor management of my health. And so, at my age-- I'm now 52, I'm attempting to reverse so much of what was done the first half of my life. But there's no sense in crying over spilled milk. The idea for me now is to go forward in an educated way regarding my health. When you know better, you should do better.

When it comes to physical fitness, when it comes to spiritual wellbeing, you must be properly educated and act upon it. Being an entrepreneur is not easy and if you don't have healthy physical and mental habits, you will break down at some point. You could have a thriving business, or a thriving ministry and it will all fall. Last year, several pastors I know died of heart attacks. Like me, they never focused on self-care. Opting instead to care for others. Yes, caring for others is noble, but the fact remains that you can't help anyone else if you can't help yourself. Sadly, those fellow brothers in ministry are no longer here.

We oversee the maintenance of our bodies. We are the managers. I want to encourage you as you read this chapter, "Take care of yourself." What good is it for us to do all this work to be an entrepreneur, to be a creative force, to be a force of change, to be a disruptor in our community, in our society and we cannot enjoy it because we've had a stroke? Or heart attack. Or we have severely damaged our bodies by developing diabetes and high blood pressure at a youthful age simply because we did not get proper diet, exercise, and rest.

And let me sit on rest for a minute. Our bodies require proper rest to restore our internal systems and refresh our minds. When we don't get proper rest, everything fails. Aside from a poor diet, we neglect ourselves in this area the most. As an entrepreneur you will need to pay close attention to your resting schedule. No one can go full speed all the time. Even Jesus rested. The scriptures give us many examples of Jesus requiring rest, but one in particular speaks to me. Mark 6:31-32, "Then, because so many people were coming and going that they did not even have a chance to eat, he said to them, "Come with me by yourselves to a quiet place and get some rest." So, they went away by themselves in a boat to a solitary place." Why did Jesus do this? He did it because these bodies require rest.

I work extremely hard. I am a workaholic. I am chronic workaholic. I will put in the hours. My team will tell you that they have received emails at 2:00 and 3:00 in the morning from me. We finally made an agreement that I will not be sending emails at 2:00 and 3:00 in the morning. I was having trouble sleeping. And I wanted someone to suffer with me. My team members became the target of my suffering. But I had to learn that it's important to get proper rest, proper exercise, and eat well-balanced meals.

Self-Care Means Saying "No"

Knowing when and how to say no is crucial. A few months ago, I prepared for a meeting that would present an opportunity almost too good to be true. There was a particular piece of property that I had been trying to acquire for quite some time and now all of a sudden, they seemed to be throwing it at me. It was almost like, "Now that you don't want me, I want you." Here's the problem with that. Sometimes you need to know how to say no. Be true to thine own self. This particular piece of property is quite large in size, right at about five and a half acres. And the now new property owners are seeking someone to take it and redevelop it. The issue I had was I currently was working on another project, and it would be too much for me to undertake at that time. When you're in business as an entrepreneur, you need to be able to determine when you've reached your max. You have to always safeguard against overload. Trying to be too many things to too many people can be catastrophic. It is better be good at one thing than be horrible at a whole lot.

So, I went into the meeting with the mindset that I really can't help these individuals. Not that I didn't want to help them, I just simply knew how to say no. Good opportunity, bad timing. As an entrepreneur, as you develop in your walk as an entrepreneur, your journey as an entrepreneur, you must be able to discern between seasons. You see, if I just take this job because it's an opportunity, I run the risk of going into overload. Overload and financial obligations and payroll and needing people and stressing my team and stressing my planning groups out all for the sake of saying, "I've got this wonderful piece of property." But the truth is, the property would be there if it's really for me when I finished the property development that I was currently on. Oftentimes, as entrepreneurs, we're trying to grab everything that comes our way. In short, it's called greed. It kills us every time. And what I want you to guard against is being greedy. Every opportunity, though it may be a good opportunity, may not be for you right now. If it's for you, put it on the shelf, wait a while, see what happens. If you approach it from a different angle. Look at it and determine the real sense of its worth, not just the fluff.

Because so many of us are caught up with the fluff. We see the glory in it. But then we discover the end results are not all they cracked up to be because we are stressed out, overtaxed and heavily burdened. It just does not work. And when you're the one that's going home with the headaches, and your blood pressure is through the roof because you're trying to figure it out, when you just could've waited a few months and let it work its own self out. Don't worry. Relax. You will get there. It's just going to take time, proper planning, and proper execution. But ultimately, you are the one that's going to determine when to say no.

When managing our businesses, we (rightly) focus on tracking things like our sales, costs and often awareness measurements. But self-care for entrepreneurs should also involve adding some checks that keep us on top of our personal wellbeing too.

Maybe there's a certain type of client that you want to avoid, or maybe you keep forgetting to eat lunch, or maybe you need to stop seeing friends so often or start seeing friends more! Only you will know what changes you need to get you operating at your best.

There's always room for improvement but making this check-in a regular part of your self-care process will give you the insights you need to make slight changes so that you're a happy and healthy entrepreneur.

Reflection Time

1. Are you eating, sleeping and exercising well? Do you feel good in your body or do you feel tired and sluggish? What's working well in this area and what could you improve on?

2. Are you thinking positively, able to access your creativity, and feeling productive? Or are you stressed, getting stuck in negative thoughts, and feeling stuck?

For more information about Dr. Patrick Sanders Sr. and this book, please send an email to <u>eldersanders@att.net</u>.

Spiritual Wisdom for Entrepreneurs

Dr. Patrick W. Sanders Sr.

Made in the USA
Middletown, DE
02 July 2019